YOUR KNOWLEDGE HAS VALUE

- We will publish your bachelor's and master's thesis, essays and papers

- Your own eBook and book - sold worldwide in all relevant shops

- Earn money with each sale

Upload your text at www.GRIN.com
and publish for free

Eddie Fisher

Tapas De Culture - A short introduction to working with International Teams

GRIN Verlag

Bibliografische Information der Deutschen Nationalbibliothek:

Die Deutsche Bibliothek verzeichnet diese Publikation in der Deutschen National-
bibliografie; detaillierte bibliografische Daten sind im Internet über http://dnb.d-
nb.de/ abrufbar.

Dieses Werk sowie alle darin enthaltenen einzelnen Beiträge und Abbildungen
sind urheberrechtlich geschützt. Jede Verwertung, die nicht ausdrücklich vom
Urheberrechtsschutz zugelassen ist, bedarf der vorherigen Zustimmung des Verla-
ges. Das gilt insbesondere für Vervielfältigungen, Bearbeitungen, Übersetzungen,
Mikroverfilmungen, Auswertungen durch Datenbanken und für die Einspeicherung
und Verarbeitung in elektronische Systeme. Alle Rechte, auch die des auszugsweisen
Nachdrucks, der fotomechanischen Wiedergabe (einschließlich Mikrokopie) sowie
der Auswertung durch Datenbanken oder ähnliche Einrichtungen, vorbehalten.

Imprint:

Copyright © 2007 GRIN Verlag GmbH
Druck und Bindung: Books on Demand GmbH, Norderstedt Germany
ISBN: 978-3-656-20693-4

This book at GRIN:

http://www.grin.com/en/e-book/112183/tapas-de-culture-a-short-introduction-to-
working-with-international-teams

GRIN - Your knowledge has value

Der GRIN Verlag publiziert seit 1998 wissenschaftliche Arbeiten von Studenten, Hochschullehrern und anderen Akademikern als eBook und gedrucktes Buch. Die Verlagswebsite www.grin.com ist die ideale Plattform zur Veröffentlichung von Hausarbeiten, Abschlussarbeiten, wissenschaftlichen Aufsätzen, Dissertationen und Fachbüchern.

Visit us on the internet:

http://www.grin.com/

http://www.facebook.com/grincom

http://www.twitter.com/grin_com

"Tapas De Culture –
A short introduction to cultural awareness and working with International Teams"

Author: Dr Eddie Fisher

Presented for the University of Brno, Czech Republic, in Ramzova in September 2007

TABLE OF CONTENTS

1. Introduction

Many companies already operate in a number of foreign countries. More are following each year. The concept of 'global working' has become an accepted modus operandi for more and more companies both in the United Kingdom and other countries. As a result, people at all levels within their organizations have opportunities to work with people from other countries. This is not an easy task and brings with it some cultural difficulties. These need to be managed carefully and with due consideration to everyone involved. According to Davison and Ward (1999) the world is becoming increasingly interconnected: the technology has allowed us to travel and talk to each other across distances; there are more of us with higher expectations; and industrialized nations have saturated their own markets. We have to work increasingly with people from other nations to solve complex international problems and to take advantage of opportunities often far away from home.

Working with people whose values and beliefs are different from your own, can often lead to costly misunderstandings and even business failures. However, when successfully managed, differences in culture can lead to innovative business practices and faster and better learning within the organization. People will get on better with their colleagues from other countries once they have learned more about cultural differences. They will learn that their own views are not the only ones, and that the variety of views coming from the different cultures can actually lead to better business solutions that are good for the benefit of everyone.

We are at an age where 'information space' is used increasingly for doing business. An adequate communications structure needs to be in place to make it work well. The physical location is of less concern than time zones (Davison and Ward, 1999).

It is imperative to understand the many ways in which cultural differences can influence the interactions within global working or interacting. Trompenaars and Hampden-Turner (1997) suggest that the culture within this environment can be visible:

- Rituals
- Clothes
- Food

Or not visible:

- Thinking
- Values
- Beliefs
- Assumptions

But consider: not every individual within any given culture will always behave exactly as the observed or perceived behaviours associated with that culture. Not everyone is the same. And some people have had exposure to working in international environments, so it is likely that they have changed their behaviour

because of local influences. Be careful not to stereotype people such as 'The
Italians are not good at planning and organizing but are good at being creative'.

2. Aim of Introduction to Cultural Awareness

This short and practical introduction has been put together to give you some basic
understanding of what culture is. It will make you more aware of the cultural
differences that exist within different cultures and what **You** can do to make it work
better for you and those you are working or going to work with.

The introduction is also meant to be a refresher for those of you who have been
working in multi-cultural environments for some time. It is valuable to take a step
back and be reminded of the cultural differences that exist within the new divisions.

The aim of this short introduction is to make you more aware of your own culture and
those of others you are working with. It is a stepping stone on the longer road to
become or be good at working and interacting with people from many countries.

This short introduction is only meant to be an appetizer. Many cultural awareness
courses are available, lasting between one and two days. These go further into the
finer details of cultural differences, combined with appropriate exercises to improve
your understanding of the subject matter. There are also many books published now.
A suggested reading list is shown at the end of this document.

Cultural differences vary from country to country. There is no right or wrong culture.
They are just different. But let's now take a closer look at what culture actually is.

3. What is Culture?

Here are some interpretations, taken from current publications, of what culture is:

- How we do things around here (Lewis, 1999)
- How people understand their world and make sense of it (Trompenaars and
  Hamden-Turner, 1997)
- Values and beliefs people hold (Davison and Ward, 1999)
- The collective programming of the mind which distinguishes the members of one
  category of people from another (Hofstede, 1980)

Do not think of cultural differences as an obstacle or hindrance. View it as an
opportunity to improve existing business practices, to make your working
relationships with people from other cultures better and to aid further learning. By
learning about the cultures of other people (how they do things around here), it is
possible to see that your own solutions may not be the only, best or most appropriate
for the task in hand.

You need to understand the 'logic' of another culture, e.g. why it is that people do
things the way they do. For example, if you arrange a meeting for 10am with Spanish

4

colleagues, do not feel offended if they are not punctual. Perhaps arrange meetings with them in such as way that there is some extra time available. It is just part of their culture. That's all.

Find points of connection and some common ground. Look at why people do things the way they do. Understanding this means that you can come up with a solution.

Values, beliefs, language and customs are all social behaviours associated with culture (Lewis, 1999). They are embedded in a particular context and are connected to other deeply held values and beliefs. We need to attend to what different things mean to different people (cultures). For example, urgent means 'immediate' to UK people but means 'as soon as possible' to an Italian. This is important for you to understand and to apply this knowledge, particularly when you manage a project team with Italy taking the lead role.

The essence of culture is the shared ways groups of people understand and interpret the world (Trompenaars and Hampden-Turner, 1997). There is a need to maintain one's own culture within a multi-cultural environment such as our truly global working environment. Ask yourself the question: how do others actually think? Then build on from here. It is this understanding of how others think that is so important to improving your cultural awareness.

The following diagram, developed by the author, illustrates how you can improve your cultural learning:

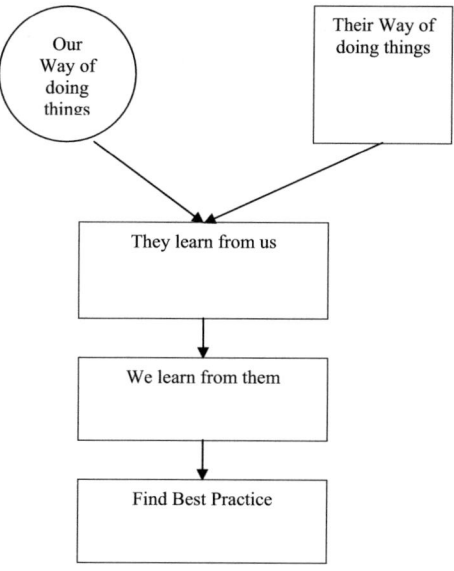

The important point here is that people will not only learn from each other but they will also learn something new.

4. Why do you think that cultural awareness is so valuable?

When you work with people from different cultures, you will observe many behaviours that are often fundamentally different from your own. Being aware of these behaviours, and that they are different from your own, is the first step towards becoming culturally aware. You are taking in what goes on around you as far as people are concerned. This is a good thing. Without people nothing goes.

In order to move things forward such as a project deadline or reach agreements on tasks (it is the 'who does what, how and by when'), you need to apply your new cultural awareness and understanding in the most appropriate way. For example, if you need to agree a plan of works and you know that Italians do not like planning too much, find another way of managing this. Involve Italian colleagues in your thinking outside of meetings, ask them for their creative inputs to find solutions to problems and then engage them to take ownership of some of the major activities.

This will appeal to Italian people. You will have them on your side. This is also good for you because you have found creative solutions to your problems, and you have a lead country to manage this for you. This worked well for me in a recent project I managed where we worked with seven Operating Companies simultaneously to find a technical solution. It was because of the creative strengths of the Italians involved that we found the most viable solution in a short period of time.

In this way you engage the various cultures in your team by using their cultural strengths and combine these with your own strengths (in this case perhaps planning and organizing) to reach your desired goals. Build on the positive strengths and ignore the negative weaknesses. Use this cultural diversity to build a strong team where everyone accepts everyone else for what they are, irrespective of where they come from.

5. National Characteristics

The following table adapted from Lewis (1999), summarizes some of the main national characteristics associated with nationals from different countries. This list is not exhaustive. Get books from your local library as suggested in the reading list at the end of this document, and read up on other cultures, depending on where your work or meetings may take you.

Country	Typical Behaviours Associated with that Culture
USA	Very informal, first name terms, use humour, put their cards on the table right from the beginning, they want 'Yes' and work out details later, they are persistent and consistent, are often blunt, assume that the American norms are the correct ones
Britain	Informal, first name terms fairly quickly, apply humour extensively, do not like to be hurried to make decisions, prefer to build long-term relationships,
Ireland	Warmly informal at all times, apply good sense of humour, not great Agenda followers in meetings, ideas are more important than facts
Germany	Hierarchical, very formal, well prepared at meetings, they tend to look for common ground, they do not like being rushed, they respect titles such as Doctor, don't like humour during business sessions, are very sincere people
Netherlands	Tolerant, conservative, frank and open, informal, consultative, innovative, consensual, dutiful
France	Formal, polite, they reveal their hand late in negotiations, dislike being rushed into making decisions, establish firm personal relationships, are very precise, walk away from the Agenda and talk at random, very logical
Italy	Charming, intelligent, excellent communicators, very flexible, like to share details of family, holidays, etc, do not believe that Italian must always be best, very emotional, do not follow Agendas, do not plan very methodically, are very people oriented, like team work
Finland	Energetic, inventive, warm-hearted, hard-working and intelligent, are not very communicative, are very uneasy with foreigners, are persistent., original thinking, are adaptable, ready to learn and compromise, are perfectionists, do not like close supervision, high on self-respect and inner harmony
Sweden	Honest, caring, well-informed, efficient, fear of confrontation, slow at decision-making, good listeners, are more deal than people oriented, very informal
Japan	Are very shy people, silence shows respect for the speaker, they do not like to offend you by showing open disagreement or refusal, often close their eyes to concentrate on what you are saying, they do not like to be rushed because they must complete their consensus, meetings are not considered to be gatherings to make decisions, they are short on words because they distrust words, often keep a straight face to be impassive(not trying to deceive you), prefer not to talk business for the first 15 minutes but like to talk about friends, family and hobbies

6. Leadership Styles and Behaviours of Different Cultures

Because of the different values and beliefs people from diverse cultures hold, it is inevitable that the leaders in these cultures also have different leadership styles or ways of making people do things. It is useful to know what these styles are so you can prepare yourself better, for example, for influencing the leaders to help you achieve the goals of your project or work, or resolving conflicts that hinder progress.

The table below, adapted from Lewis (1999), gives you a brief summary of the leadership styles you may encounter. Before you look at these, let me give you a personal example how, for example, understanding the German leadership styles helped me to get what I needed for one of my programmes.

I was waiting for vital network security information from the Head of Security of one of the Operating Companies. Despite a couple of reminders by phone and E-mail to forward me the requested information, I did not receive the information I requested within the required time-scale. I then changed my approach. I **told** him that I needed the information by 2pm on that day (not **asked** him this time). Within a few hours I received what I had been asking for quite some time. I used my authority as Senior Programme Manager in a direct and clear communication. This also fitted in with his own organisational and hierarchical set-up. In this case, my approach of 'Give him an order and he will do' worked well.

Country	Leadership Styles and Behavioural Characteristics
Germany	Hierarchical but often reaching consensus from involvement of lower level staff, believe in order via sufficient rules, regulations and procedures, clear chain of command in each department and information and instructions are passed down from the top
France	Even more autocratic than Germany, only top management makes important decisions
Britain	Could be described as diplomatic, tactful, laid back, casual, reasonable, helpful and willing to compromise
USA	Speed is of essence, acting individually and in their own interests, being tough and risk-taking, leaders are assertive and aggressive
Sweden	Democratic and de-centralized leadership, consensus reaching with most staff before making decisions, obsession with people orientation often leads to delay in making decisions

7. Examples from a real global project- and why you should follow these….

I am now going to draw on some personal experiences from a project I managed recently within our global environment. I want to share these experiences with you because they will help you to turn theory into practice. And remember: the more you practise the better you will get.

a). When I recently organized the project kick-off meeting for another Phase within one of my programmes, I took the time to read up on the Austrian culture and their management/leadership styles. Loaded with this information, I planned my approach how to best address the new team at the meeting.

I welcomed everyone personally, exchanging business cards and recognizing their title, role and qualifications openly, introducing some basic humour to break the ice.

I started the formal meeting by praising their leader for the good work they had already done to make a service launch by 30 June 2003 possible. I also showed appreciation for the work everyone else had been engaged in to make this happen.

My approach worked well. The new team members felt valued for what they are and for their contributions made so far. Building rapport in this way helped me to gain their trust and commitment and respect.

b.) Global project or work environments often require strong leadership to drive things through. When representatives from many different countries get together to design develop and implement, for example, a new system, it is inevitable that there will be differences of opinion. The two senior managers in this programme (including myself) used their knowledge of the cultural differences to good effect. We knew that the Italians did not want to plan too much, that the Germans wanted to plan everything 100 %, with the rest somewhere in–between.

As a compromise, we used the Italian strength of being innovative to drive through new ideas. We used the German excellence at planning and organizing to help with the production of a global Master Plan and we used the other values of the other countries to drive through changes, often at short notice. It worked very well.

Involving everyone for what they stood for made the team rise above the rest and deliver the solutions within agreed time-scales. The application of this cultural awareness made it all happen.

c.) I recommend that you take time up-front and meet with the key players of your project or work **before** any kick-off meetings or decision-making meetings. E-mail, phone or video links are never as effective as personal face to face meetings (in the case of representatives from Australia/New Zealand, for example, consider to combine a number of meetings so you can justify the expense/time spent).

I did this at the beginning of one of the programme phases. It proved invaluable to meet face to face to discuss and resolve issues immediately. Having held direct personal and business talks with project managers from these countries was essential to their successful launch. Because we had to stay overnight, this was an opportunity to get to know people better. We talked about our families, hobbies and so on.

When we had conflict situations much later in the programme, I was able to use the conflict constructively to improve, for example, technical solutions for the project. I would not have been able to do this without the prior face to face and off-line meetings that we had. The human interaction during face to face meetings cannot be replaced by phone calls or E-mails or video links. But use these as tools for follow-ups or during later stages of your work or project. They should be used to complement each other.

Always be honest with yourself and accept yourself for what you are. Do the same for people from other cultures. Listen to them actively, checking from time to time that you really understand what they are telling you. Paraphrase if necessary to aid your understanding. Understand where they are coming from. What is it that makes them 'tick'? What is important to them? Do not try to change the behaviour of people from other cultures, accept them for what they are and then keep working with this understanding.

d.) Another piece of advice: Once you got to know the key players in your team, use conference calls as a means to resolve issues and conflicts. I often found in my programme that E-mails (technical issues) were getting longer and longer, with more and more people being copied in.

Find out who the key decision makers are in each company and 'what makes them tick'
(what is important to them). Then prepare a clear agenda, stating the purpose of the call and the desired outcomes. For example, state that a decision is required whether to connect the new network via the Internet or using a VPN solution.

This will give you a good chance to move things forward quickly and stop the team members from wasting their valuable time. It is a good way of engaging them in the work/project. But remember to value the cultural differences.

d.) Meetings: Most of my project meetings in my programme did not start on time. I planned for this by preparing an agenda in such a way that I could recover lost time reasonably well. This is what I did. I considered that people from Germany like to start punctually. They tend to have formal introductions, sit down and begin the meeting. People from the UK like to have some small talk first, a cup of tea and then casually begin the meeting. Italians and Spanish people like to have some lengthy small talks first (10-20 minutes), then start when everyone else has arrived. Other cultures fit in somewhere in-between.

I often used compromises to meet everyone's requirements. Start the small talk earlier, as soon as the first people arrive. Also use this time wisely to perhaps discuss your issues with people prior to the meeting to gain support. Start the meeting within 15 minutes of the arranged time or whenever the key players have arrived. Do not wait until everyone has arrived, they may be delayed at the airport. You can always recap later.

You cannot get it absolutely right for everyone so use common sense and tell people what you are going to do. Remember also that many people have been working in an international environment for some time now and have probably changed their normal behaviour to fit in with the rest.

I have summarized some basic points of things to think about before engaging in some activities such as informal talks and sending E-mails:

Activity	What To Do	Done
Planning of cross-cultural meetings	1.Check which nationalities will attend, then read up on the cultural differences of these to prepare yourself	Y/N
	2. Check if they usually start on time or if they have small talks first, then set the Agenda and the starting time accordingly	Y/N
	3. Check if they make decisions at meetings or if they must check with others first, then decide whom to invite so that the desired decisions can be made at your meeting and do not need to be referred to another person, adding further delay	Y/N
	4. Encourage native English speakers to slow down and paraphrase, if necessary, so you all understand what each other is saying	Y/N
	5. Do some preparation work to find out a little bit about the cultures you are going to meet with	Y/N
	6. Make sure you provide food and drinks in line with the cultural needs of attendees such as no alcohol, vegetarian or vegan snacks, and so on	Y/N

Telephone Calls	1.Speak slowly if the other person is not a natural English speaker	Y/N
	2.Check your understanding of what is being said and /or agreed from time to time	Y/N
	3. Consider the time difference, particularly for early morning, lunch time and late evening calls	Y/N
	4.Small talk first if the other person is from a culture where this is expected, such as Italy, Spain or UK	Y/N
E-mails	1.Be precise and clear in your communications, remember not to write anything that could offend the other culture	Y/N
	2.Do not use E-mail unless you have to send a document, or the other culture prefers to work using this medium. Pick up the phone and talk instead, or have a short meeting where practical	Y/N
	3.Use English that can be understood by people who are not native English speakers, avoid jargon or slang	Y/N
Informal Talks	1.Have informal talks with people from other cultures as much as you can, instead of E-mails and formal communications	Y/N
	2.Share details of hobbies, friends and family	Y/N
	3.Have a chat over coffee, or in the corridor, to discuss business matters in an	Y/N

| | informal environment, or on neutral ground | |
| | 4. Read up on which cultures prefer informal talks, then act accordingly | Y/N |

8. List of Recommendations suggested by the author: Do's and Don'ts

Do	Do Not
-Accept people for what they are	-Try to change people
-Respect the culture of others	-Force people to work against their cultural upbringing
-Know or get to know your own culture	-Ignore the status/rank or professional qualification of people from different cultures
-Read up on cultural differences and prepare yourself well before meetings	-Criticise other cultures within your team, such as the Spanish are always late for meetings)
-Find out the strong points of each culture and use this to your advantage to deliver your goals	-Express a preference of one culture over another
-Get to know the people better, have lunch or dinner together	-Patronise people by treating them as if they are inferior to your culture
-arrange a private function such as bowling to celebrate successes with the team	-Use humour unless you are sure that it does not offend anyone(if you are not sure, leave it out until you are more established as a team)
	-Ignore suggestions from smaller companies/countries because they are less developed

9. Summary

I hope that this short introduction has increased your level of cultural awareness, and given you an incentive to do even more. It is not aimed to turn you into a cultural expert over night. It will take some time before you become better at managing the cultural differences when working with people from different cultural backgrounds to your own. It is a journey, and you have perhaps just taken the first steps on the long road to becoming culturally aware.

I used real life practical examples and combined these with Data from empirical research that has been carried out by a number of professional bodies that specialize in cultural awareness.

There is one clear message that I wish to get across to you: improve your cultural awareness and you will succeed in working well with people from other cultures. Those who accept the opinions and manners of others as being at least equally valid, if not occasionally superior, will be able to enhance the team spirits within their work areas and thus achieve their goals much better.

Being culturally aware is an essential ingredient of managing and working with/in international teams successfully.

10. Suggested Reading List

To have cultural awareness and understanding and apply this is essential in today's global business environments. The following books will help you to deepen your knowledge in this area. This list is not exhaustive. Your local library will also have the latest publications that cover this subject matter.

Morrison, Terri; Conway, Wayne and Borden, George(1994). *Kiss, Bow or Shake Hands*, Holbrook, MA: Adams Media Corporation

Lewis, Richard. D (1996,1999).*When Cultures Collide*, Nicholas Brealey Publishing Ltd.

Axtell, Roger E (ed., 1985).*Do's and Taboos Around The World*, compiled by the Parker Pen Company

Mole, John(1995).*Mind Your Manners: Managing Business Cultures in Europe*, London: Nicholas Brealey

Trompenaars, Fons and Hampden-Turner, Charles(1997).*Riding the Waves of Culture: Understanding Cultural Diversity in Business*, 2nd Edition, London: Nicholas Brealey

11. References

Canney Davison,S. and Ward, K. (1999). *Leading International Teams*, McGraw-Hill Publishing Company

Hofstede, G.(1980).*Culture's Consequences: International Differences in Work-Related Values,* Newbury Park, CA:Sage

Lewis, R.D.(1999).*When Cultures Collide*, Nicholas Brealey Publishing

Trompenaars, F. and Hampden-Turner, C.(1997).*Riding the Waves Of Culture-Understanding Cultural Diversity in Business*, Second Edition, Nicholas Brealey Publishing